GET RICH NOW

Secrets to Building Wealth and Living Your Dream Life

JOY DANIELS

Copyright © 2023 by Joy Daniels

TABLE OF CONTENT

INTRODUCTION

Welcome to "Get Rich Now: Secrets to Building Wealth and Living Your Dream Life," a groundbreaking guide that transcends traditional financial advice to unlock the secrets of true prosperity. In a world buzzing with get-rich-quick schemes, this book stands as a beacon of practical wisdom, offering actionable insights and a roadmap to financial success tailored to the modern era.

In these pages, you will embark on a transformative journey that goes beyond mere wealth accumulation. This book delves into the psychology of wealth, empowering you to cultivate the mindset of a successful individual. Drawing on a wealth of research and real-life examples, it unveils the hidden principles that distinguish the affluent from the rest, guiding you on a path of abundance.

"Get Rich Now" demystifies the complexities of personal finance, making it accessible to readers of all backgrounds. Whether you're a seasoned investor or a financial novice, this book provides a comprehensive toolkit for building and preserving wealth. From savvy investment strategies to practical budgeting tips, each chapter is a stepping stone towards financial mastery.

Moreover, this book doesn't merely focus on amassing wealth for its own sake. It encourages you to envision and create your dream life. Through inspiring anecdotes and case studies, you'll discover how individuals have turned their financial success into a means to lead fulfilling, purpose-driven lives. The book underscores the importance of aligning your financial goals with your passions, fostering a holistic approach to prosperity that extends beyond the balance sheet.

"Get Rich Now" is not just a book; it's a blueprint for transforming your financial reality and achieving the lifestyle you've always envisioned. Join me on this enlightening journey, and let's unlock the secrets to building wealth and living your dream life together.

CHAPTER 1: MINDSET MATTERS

Welcome to Chapter 1: "Mindset Matters," the foundational cornerstone of your journey towards financial abundance and a life of prosperity. In this chapter, we will delve into the intricate realm of the psychology of wealth, unravelling the profound impact that one's mindset can have on financial success. As you embark on this enlightening exploration, you'll discover that the road to riches is not merely paved with monetary strategies but is equally shaped by the beliefs and attitudes harbored within.

This chapter serves as a compass, guiding you through the labyrinth of limiting beliefs that may have hindered your financial growth in the past. We will explore the power of positive thinking and its transformative influence on your approach to wealth creation. By the end of this section, you'll not only understand the importance of cultivating a success-oriented mindset but also gain practical tools to reframe your thoughts and align them with your financial goals.

Prepare to challenge preconceived notions and embrace a new perspective on wealth. "Mindset Matters" is your gateway to unlocking the hidden potential within, setting the stage for a paradigm shift that will resonate throughout the entirety of your financial journey. Let's delve into the fascinating world of your thoughts and beliefs, and together, let's pave the way for a mindset that propels you towards lasting financial success.

- Unveiling the Psychology of Wealth

The psychology of wealth explores the intricate relationship between individuals' mental attitudes, emotions, and behaviors concerning money and financial success. It acknowledges that one's mindset plays a pivotal role in shaping financial outcomes, often influencing decisions related to earning, spending, saving, and investing. Several key aspects characterize the psychology of wealth:

1. Mindset and Beliefs:

- *Scarcity vs. Abundance:* Individuals with a scarcity mindset often focus on limitations and fear of lack, while those with an abundance mindset believe in opportunities and possibilities.

- *Limiting Beliefs:* Negative beliefs about money inherited from upbringing or cultural influences can hinder financial growth. Identifying and challenging these beliefs is crucial for change.

2. Risk Perception and Decision-Making:

- *Risk Aversion:* The fear of financial loss can lead to conservative decision-making. Understanding and managing risk is essential for successful wealth building.

- *Behavioral Biases:* Cognitive biases, such as loss aversion and herd mentality, can impact investment choices. Recognizing and mitigating these biases is crucial for sound financial decisions.

3. Delayed Gratification and Discipline:

- *Instant Gratification:* A challenge for many individuals is the temptation of immediate rewards over long-term gains. Developing discipline and embracing delayed gratification are essential for building wealth.

4. Self-Worth and Money:

- *Money Scripts:* Personal beliefs about self-worth and deservingness impact financial choices. Positive self-perception often correlates with a healthier approach to money.

5. Financial Goal Setting and Visualization:

- *Goal Alignment:* Aligning financial goals with personal values and life aspirations enhances motivation and commitment.

- *Visualization Techniques:* Imagining and visualizing financial success can positively influence behavior and goal achievement.

6. Lifestyle Inflation and Hedonic Adaptation:

- *Lifestyle Creep:* As income rises, so do expenses. Being mindful of lifestyle inflation helps maintain a sustainable financial trajectory.

- *Hedonic Adaptation:* The tendency to return to a baseline level of happiness after positive or negative changes underscores the importance of intentional spending.

Understanding the psychology of wealth empowers individuals to make informed financial decisions and fosters a positive relationship with money. By addressing and reshaping mental attitudes and behaviors, individuals can create a mindset conducive to building lasting wealth and achieving their financial aspirations.

- Overcoming Limiting Beliefs

Overcoming limiting beliefs is a crucial step in fostering a positive mindset and unlocking one's full potential for financial success. These beliefs, often ingrained in our subconscious, can act as barriers to personal and financial growth. Here's a process to help overcome limiting beliefs:

1. Identity Limiting Beliefs:

- *Self-Reflection:* Take time to reflect on your thoughts and attitudes towards money. Identify recurring negative beliefs or patterns that may be holding you back.

- *Journaling:* Keep a journal to record your thoughts and feelings about money. This can provide clarity on underlying beliefs and their origins.

2. Challenge and Question:

- *Rational Examination:* Question the validity of your limiting beliefs. Ask yourself if these beliefs are based on facts or if they are assumptions that can be challenged.

- *Seek Evidence to the Contrary:* Look for examples of individuals who have overcome similar circumstances or challenges. This can provide evidence that contradicts negative beliefs.

3. **Cognitive Restructuring:**

- *Positive Affirmations:* Replace negative thoughts with positive affirmations. Affirmations help rewire the brain and reinforce a more optimistic and empowering mindset.

- *Visualization Techniques:* Envision yourself breaking free from limiting beliefs and achieving financial success. Visualization can make these positive outcomes more tangible and achievable.

4. **Educate Yourself:**

- *Financial Literacy:* Enhance your understanding of personal finance and wealth-building strategies. Education can empower you with the knowledge needed to challenge and change limiting beliefs.

- *Role Models:* Learn from the experiences of individuals who have overcome financial challenges. Reading success stories and biographies can provide inspiration and practical insights.

5. **Set Realistic Goals:**

- *Incremental Steps:* Break down larger financial goals into smaller, manageable steps. Achieving these smaller milestones builds confidence and disproves limiting beliefs.

- *Track Progress:* Keep track of your financial progress. Celebrate achievements, no matter how small, to reinforce positive beliefs about your capabilities.

6. **Surround Yourself with Positivity:**

- *Supportive Networks:* Engage with individuals who share positive attitudes towards money and success. Surrounding yourself with a supportive network can reinforce positive beliefs.

- *Limit Negative Influences:* Minimize exposure to negativity, whether it's from people, media, or other sources. Choose content and relationships that uplift and inspire.

7. Seek Professional Help:

- *Therapy or Coaching:* If limiting beliefs are deeply ingrained or significantly impacting your life, consider seeking the guidance of a therapist or a coach specializing in mindset and financial empowerment.

Overcoming limiting beliefs is an ongoing process that requires self-awareness, commitment, and continuous effort. By actively challenging and reshaping negative thoughts, individuals can pave the way for a mindset conducive to financial success and personal fulfilment.

- Cultivating a Success-Oriented Mindset

Cultivating a success-oriented mindset is a transformative process that involves fostering positive attitudes, beliefs, and habits to propel oneself towards personal and financial achievement. Here's a step-by-step guide to help you cultivate a success-oriented mindset:

1. Define Your Vision:

- *Clarity of Goals:* Clearly articulate your personal and financial goals. Define what success means to you, both in the short term and long term.

- *Vision Board:* Create a vision board that visually represents your goals and aspirations. This tangible representation can serve as a daily reminder of your vision.

2. Positive Affirmations:

- *Affirmative Language:* Replace negative self-talk with positive affirmations. Use statements that reinforce your capabilities, strengths, and the belief that success is achievable.

- *Daily Affirmation Routine:* Incorporate a daily routine where you repeat affirmations aloud. Consistency is key to rewiring your subconscious mind.

3. Embrace a Growth Mindset:

- Learn from Challenges: View challenges as opportunities for growth rather than insurmountable obstacles. Embrace setbacks as valuable lessons that contribute to your personal development.

- Continuous Learning: Cultivate a thirst for knowledge. Stay curious, seek new skills, and approach every experience as a chance to expand your capabilities.

4. Visualization Techniques:

- Mental Rehearsal: Visualize your success. Imagine yourself achieving your goals and experiencing the emotions associated with that success. This mental rehearsal primes your mind for positive outcomes.

- Create a Mental Movie: Develop a vivid mental image of your success story. Play this mental movie regularly to reinforce your belief in your ability to achieve your goals.

5. Surround Yourself with Positivity:

- Choose Positive Influences: Surround yourself with individuals who uplift and inspire you. Positive relationships contribute to a supportive environment that reinforces your success-oriented mindset.

- Limit Negativity: Minimize exposure to negative influences, whether they come from people, media, or your thoughts. Focus on creating a positive and empowering mental space.

6. Celebrate Small Wins:

- Acknowledge Achievements: Celebrate even the smallest successes along your journey. Acknowledging and appreciating your progress reinforces a positive mindset and motivates continued effort.

- Gratitude Practice: Develop a gratitude mindset by regularly reflecting on and expressing gratitude for the positive aspects of your life.

7. **Create a Success Ritual:**

- *Morning Routine:* Establish a morning routine that sets a positive tone for the day. This might include affirmations, visualization, or activities that bring you joy and motivation.

- *Reflect and Plan:* End each day with reflection. Acknowledge your achievements, learn from challenges, and plan for the next steps in your success journey.

8. **Resilience in the Face of Failure:**

- *Reframe Failure:* See failure as a temporary setback rather than a reflection of your worth. Embrace resilience and learn from failures to enhance your future success.

- *Adaptability:* Develop the ability to adapt to change and bounce back from setbacks. Flexibility and resilience are integral components of a success-oriented mindset.

Cultivating a success-oriented mindset is an ongoing process that requires dedication and self-awareness. By consciously shaping your thoughts, beliefs, and actions, you can create a mindset that propels you towards the fulfilment of your goals and a life of sustained success.

CHAPTER 2:

FINANCIAL

FOUNDATIONS

Welcome to Chapter 2: "Financial Foundations," where we embark on a journey to build the solid groundwork necessary for a prosperous and sustainable financial future. In this chapter, we will delve into the fundamental principles of personal finance, laying the groundwork for sound money management and wealth creation. Just as a sturdy building requires a robust foundation, your financial success hinges on establishing and fortifying these essential pillars.

Financial Foundations serves as a compass, guiding you through the intricacies of budgeting, saving, and understanding the critical aspects of credit and debt management. As we navigate through these key elements, you will gain insights into the practical strategies that underpin a secure financial structure.

This chapter isn't just about numbers; it's about empowerment. By mastering the basics of financial management, you gain control over your financial destiny, fostering a sense of security and confidence. Whether you're starting your financial journey or seeking to reinforce your existing knowledge, the insights within this chapter will equip you with the tools needed to navigate the ever-changing landscape of personal finance.

Get ready to explore the building blocks of financial success. From creating a budget that aligns with your goals to understand the significance of an emergency fund, Financial Foundations will provide you with the knowledge and skills to make informed decisions that resonate with your unique financial aspirations. Join me in unravelling the intricacies of financial stability, and let's construct a foundation that supports a lifetime of wealth and well-being.

- Mastering the Basics of Budgeting

Mastering the basics of budgeting is a foundational step toward financial well-being and building wealth. A budget serves as a roadmap for your finances, helping you allocate resources wisely, save for future goals, and avoid unnecessary debt. Here's a step-by-step guide to help you master the basics of budgeting:

1. **Set Clear Financial Goals:**

 - *Short-Term and Long-Term Goals:* Identify your financial objectives, whether they're short-term (e.g., paying off debt) or long-term (e.g., buying a home, saving for retirement). These goals will shape your budgeting priorities.

2. **Calculate Your Income:**

 - *Sources of Income:* List all sources of income, including your salary, bonuses, freelance work, or any other consistent revenue streams.

- *Net Income:* Determine your net income by subtracting taxes and other deductions. This is the amount you have available for budgeting.

3. **List Your Expenses:**

- *Fixed Expenses:* Identify essential fixed expenses like rent or mortgage, utilities, insurance, and loan payments.

- *Variable Expenses:* List variable expenses such as groceries, dining out, entertainment, and transportation. Review past spending to estimate these amounts accurately.

4. **Categorize Your Spending:**

- *Needs vs. Wants:* Categorize your expenses into needs (essential) and wants (non-essential). This distinction helps prioritize spending based on importance.

5. **Create a Budget:**

- *Allocate Income:* Allocate your net income to cover your expenses. Start with necessities and then allocate funds for discretionary spending.

- Emergency Fund: Set aside a portion of your income for an emergency fund. This acts as a financial safety net for unexpected expenses.

6. **Monitor and Adjust:**

- Regularly Track Expenses: Keep a close eye on your spending throughout the month. Utilize budgeting apps or spreadsheets to monitor transactions.

- Adjust as Needed: If you overspend in one category, compensate by reducing spending in another. Flexibility is key to maintaining a realistic budget.

7. **Prioritize Debt Repayment:**

- List Debts: If you have outstanding debts, list them and prioritize repayment. Allocate a portion of your budget to clearing debts systematically.

- Snowball or Avalanche Method: Choose a debt repayment strategy that suits your preferences— either the snowball method (paying off smaller

debts first) or the avalanche method (tackling higher-interest debts first).

8. Save and Invest:

- *Establish Savings Goals:* Allocate a portion of your budget for savings, including both short-term and long-term goals.

- *Emergency Fund:* Build and maintain an emergency fund equivalent to three to six months of living expenses.

- *Invest for the Future:* Consider investing for long-term goals, such as retirement, through avenues like employer-sponsored plans or individual retirement accounts (IRAs).

9. Review and Reflect:

- *Monthly Reviews:* Regularly review your budget to ensure alignment with your financial goals. Adjust as needed to accommodate changes in income, expenses, or goals.

By mastering the basics of budgeting, you gain control over your finances, reduce stress, and create a pathway to achieving your financial objectives. Remember, budgeting is a dynamic process that evolves with your life, so stay committed and adapt as needed to ensure long-term financial success.

- Building a Solid Emergency Fund

Building a solid emergency fund is a crucial component of financial stability and resilience. An emergency fund acts as a financial safety net, providing a buffer against unexpected expenses or sudden changes in income. Follow these steps to effectively build and maintain a robust emergency fund:

1. **Set a Target Amount:**

   - *Calculate Living Expenses:* Determine your monthly living expenses, including rent or mortgage, utilities, groceries, insurance, and other essential costs.

- *Establish a Goal:* Aim to save three to six months' worth of living expenses. This target provides a sufficient cushion to cover financial emergencies.

2. Prioritize Emergency Fund Contributions:

- *Make it a Budget Priority:* Allocate a specific portion of your monthly budget to your emergency fund. Treat it as a non-negotiable expense to ensure consistent contributions.

- *Automate Savings:* Set up automatic transfers to your emergency fund each month. Automation fosters discipline and ensures regular contributions.

3. Choose the Right Savings Vehicle:

- *Liquid and Accessible:* Opt for a savings account or a money market account for your emergency fund. These accounts are easily accessible, providing liquidity in times of need.

- *Separate Accounts:* Consider opening a separate account dedicated solely to your emergency fund to avoid accidental spending.

4. Start Small, Scale Gradually:

- *Begin Gradually:* If saving a significant amount seems daunting, start small. Begin with a modest goal and gradually increase the amount as your financial situation improves.

- *Celebrate Milestones:* Acknowledge and celebrate reaching milestones, such as saving one month's worth of expenses. Positive reinforcement can motivate continued efforts.

5. Windfalls and Bonuses:

- *Allocate Windfalls:* Direct unexpected income, such as tax refunds, bonuses, or gifts, toward your emergency fund. This accelerates the growth of your safety net.

- *Avoid Lifestyle Inflation:* Resist the urge to increase spending when receiving windfalls. Use these funds to strengthen your financial foundation instead.

6. Review and Adjust:

- *Regular Assessments:* Periodically reassess your living expenses and adjust your emergency fund target if necessary. Life changes, such as a new job or family addition, may warrant adjustments.

- *Adapt to Changes:* If your financial situation changes, such as a decrease in income, consider increasing your emergency fund to ensure continued security.

7. Use Wisely, Replenish Promptly:

- *Emergency-Only Expenses:* Reserve the fund for genuine emergencies, such as medical expenses, car repairs, or job loss. Avoid using it for non-essential purchases.

- *Prompt Replenishment:* If you do dip into the emergency fund, prioritize replenishing it as soon as possible. This ensures its readiness for the next unforeseen circumstance.

8. Emergency Fund as a Financial Foundation:

- *Peace of Mind:* Recognize the psychological benefit of having a well-funded emergency fund. It provides peace of mind and reduces financial stress.

- *Protects Against Debt:* An emergency fund serves as a first line of defense against resorting to high-interest debt to cover unexpected expenses.

Building a solid emergency fund requires commitment, consistency, and strategic financial planning. By prioritizing this fundamental aspect of personal finance, you enhance your financial security and create a foundation for long-term economic well-being.

- Credit and Debt Management

Credit and debt management are critical aspects of personal finance that significantly impact one's financial health. Effectively managing credit and debt requires a combination of financial literacy, strategic planning, and disciplined decision-making. Let's comprehensively discuss these key elements:

Credit Management:

1. Understanding Credit:

- *Credit Scores:* Learn about credit scores and how they are calculated. A higher credit score increases your likelihood of favorable loan terms and lower interest rates.

- *Credit Reports:* Regularly check your credit reports for accuracy. Identify and dispute any errors promptly.

2. Establishing Credit:

- *Opening Accounts:* Initiate responsible credit behavior by opening credit accounts, such as credit cards or instalment loans.

- *Secured Credit Cards:* If new to credit, consider using secured credit cards to build a positive credit history.

3. **Maintaining a Healthy Credit Score:**

- *Timely Payments:* Pay bills and credit obligations on time to establish a positive payment history.

- *Credit Utilization:* Keep credit card balances below 30% of the available limit to maintain a favorable credit utilization ratio.

4. **Strategic Credit Usage:**

- *Appropriate Debt Levels:* Avoid accumulating unnecessary debt. Use credit responsibly and only for essential purchases.

- *Diversification:* Have a mix of credit types, including credit cards, instalment loans, and mortgages.

5. **Credit Monitoring:**

- *Regular Checkups:* Monitor your credit score regularly using reputable platforms. Some credit cards offer free credit score monitoring.

- *Identity Theft Protection:* Consider identity theft protection services to safeguard against fraudulent activity.

Debt Management:

1. Differentiating Between Good and Bad Debt:

- *Good Debt:* Investments that may appreciate over time, such as a mortgage or student loans.

- *Bad Debt:* High-interest, non-appreciating debts, like credit card balances for non-essential purchases.

2. Creating a Debt Repayment Plan:

- *Prioritize High-Interest Debt:* Focus on paying off high-interest debt first to minimize interest payments.

- *Snowball or Avalanche Method:* Choose a debt repayment strategy, either paying off the smallest debts first (snowball) or tackling the highest-interest debts (avalanche).

3. **Budgeting for Debt Repayment:**

- *Allocate Funds:* Allocate a portion of your budget specifically for debt repayment. Ensure minimum payments are made on all debts while focusing additional funds on one debt at a time.

4. **Negotiating with Creditors:**

- *Interest Rate Negotiation:* Contact creditors to negotiate lower interest rates, especially if you have a good payment history.

- *Debt Settlement:* Explore debt settlement options if you're struggling to meet your obligations.

5. **Seeking Professional Assistance:**

- *Credit Counseling:* Consult with credit counselling agencies for guidance on debt management plans.

- *Debt Consolidation:* Consider debt consolidation as a way to streamline payments and potentially reduce interest rates.

6. Avoiding Debt Traps:

- *Responsible Credit Card Use:* Use credit cards wisely to avoid accumulating high-interest debt.

- *Emergency Fund:* Maintain an emergency fund to reduce reliance on credit for unexpected expenses.

7. Learning from Mistakes:

- *Financial Education:* Use past debt experiences as lessons for financial education. Develop strategies to avoid similar situations in the future.

Effectively managing credit and debt is an ongoing process that requires diligence and adaptability. By maintaining a healthy credit profile, using credit strategically, and implementing proactive debt management strategies, individuals can achieve financial stability and work toward their long-term financial goals.

CHAPTER 3:

INVESTING INSIGHTS

Welcome to Chapter 3: "Investing Insights," a pivotal section that ventures into the dynamic world of wealth creation through strategic investments. In this chapter, we will unravel the intricacies of investing, offering valuable insights and practical wisdom to guide you on a journey towards financial growth and prosperity. Investing is not just about numbers; it's about understanding the markets, making informed decisions, and aligning your investments with your unique financial goals.

Investing Insights acts as a beacon in the vast landscape of investment opportunities, providing you with a comprehensive understanding of the principles that underpin successful investing. From navigating diverse investment vehicles to developing a sound investment strategy, this chapter is designed to empower you with the knowledge and confidence needed to navigate the ever-evolving financial markets.

As we explore various investment avenues, you will gain insights into the factors influencing market trends, risk management strategies, and the art of building a diversified portfolio. Whether you're a seasoned investor or stepping into the world of investing for the first time, Investing Insights will equip you with the tools to make informed decisions and optimize your financial future.

Get ready to demystify the complexities of investing, uncover the secrets of financial markets, and embark on a journey of wealth creation. Join me as we delve into Investing Insights, where knowledge meets action, and your financial aspirations take root. Together, let's unlock the potential of strategic investing and pave the way for a prosperous financial future.

- Navigating the World of Investments

Navigating the world of investments is an exciting yet intricate journey that requires careful consideration, strategic planning, and a deep understanding of the financial landscape. Whether you're a novice investor or have some experience, here's a comprehensive guide to help you navigate the diverse world of investments:

1. **Define Your Investment Goals:**

   - *Short-Term and Long-Term Objectives:* Clearly articulate your investment goals. Are you saving for a home, planning for retirement, or looking for short-term gains? Define both short-term and long-term objectives.

2. **Risk Tolerance and Time Horizon:**

   - *Assess Risk Tolerance:* Understand your risk tolerance—your ability and willingness to withstand market fluctuations. This will influence your investment choices.

 - *Consider Time Horizon:* Determine your investment time horizon. Different goals may have varying timeframes, impacting the appropriate investment strategies.

3. Educate Yourself:

 - *Understand Investment Vehicles:* Learn about various investment options, including stocks, bonds, mutual funds, exchange-traded funds (ETFs), real estate, and more.

 - *Financial Literacy:* Enhance your financial literacy by reading books, articles, and reputable financial news sources. Attend seminars or workshops to deepen your knowledge.

4. Diversification Strategies:

 - *Spread Your Investments:* Diversify your portfolio to spread risk. Avoid putting all your funds into a single asset class or investment.

- *Asset Allocation:* Determine the right mix of assets based on your goals and risk tolerance. This may involve balancing stocks, bonds, and other investment classes.

5. **Investment Research:**

- *Fundamental Analysis:* Conduct fundamental analysis to evaluate the financial health of companies if you're considering individual stocks.

- *Technical Analysis:* Explore technical analysis if you're interested in market trends and price movements.

6. **Risk Management:**

- *Set Stop-Loss Limits:* Establish stop-loss limits to mitigate potential losses. This involves pre-determining the point at which you would sell an investment to cut losses.

- *Regular Portfolio Reviews:* Periodically review and rebalance your portfolio to ensure it aligns with your risk tolerance and goals.

7. Choose the Right Investment Platform:

- *Brokerage Accounts:* Select a reputable brokerage platform that aligns with your investment goals. Consider fees, user interface, and available investment options.

- *Robo-Advisors:* Explore robo-advisors for a more hands-off approach to investing. These platforms use algorithms to manage portfolios based on your risk tolerance.

8. Start with Simplicity:

- *Index Funds and ETFs:* Consider low-cost index funds and ETFs, especially for beginners. These passively managed funds offer diversification and often have lower fees.

- *Gradual Entry:* Start with a manageable investment amount. As you gain confidence and experience, you can consider more sophisticated strategies.

9. **Stay Informed and Adapt:**

  - *Market Conditions:* Stay informed about global economic trends, geopolitical events, and market conditions that may impact your investments.

  - *Continuous Learning:* Investing is dynamic. Continuously educate yourself, adapt to market changes, and refine your investment strategy.

10. **Seek Professional Advice When Needed:**

  - *Financial Advisors:* Consider seeking advice from financial advisors, especially for complex financial goals or when navigating unfamiliar investment territories.

  - *Stay Active in Decision-Making:* While seeking advice is valuable, stay actively involved in decision-making to align investments with your goals and values.

Navigating the world of investments is an ongoing process that involves a combination of research, analysis, and adaptability. By approaching investment decisions with careful consideration and a commitment to continuous learning, you can build a portfolio that aligns with your financial goals and withstands the complexities of the ever-evolving market.

- Creating a Diversified Portfolio

Creating a diversified portfolio is a fundamental strategy for managing risk and optimizing returns in the world of investments. Diversification involves spreading your investments across different asset classes, industries, geographic regions, and investment types to reduce exposure to any single risk. Here's a comprehensive guide to the process of creating a diversified portfolio:

1. **Define Your Investment Goals and Risk Tolerance:**

   - Clearly outline your short-term and long-term investment goals.

- Assess your risk tolerance, considering factors such as your age, financial situation, and comfort level with market volatility.

2. Understand Asset Classes:

- Learn about various asset classes, including:

- Equities (Stocks): Represent ownership in a company.

- Fixed-Income (Bonds): Debt securities that pay periodic interest.

- Cash and Cash Equivalents: Highly liquid and low-risk assets.

- Real Assets: Physical assets like real estate and commodities.

3. Determine Asset Allocation:

- Allocate your assets based on your risk tolerance and investment goals.

- Consider a balanced mix of stocks, bonds, and other asset classes that align with your objectives.

4. Sector and Industry Diversification:

- Avoid overconcentration in a specific sector or industry.

- Allocate investments across different sectors to reduce the impact of downturns in any one industry.

5. Geographic Diversification:

- Spread investments across different geographic regions and countries.

- Global diversification helps mitigate risks associated with economic and geopolitical events in a specific region.

6. Diversify Within Asset Classes:

- Within equities, diversify across:

- Market Capitalization: Large-cap, mid-cap, and small-cap stocks.

- Geographic Regions: Domestic and international stocks.

- Sectors and Industries: Technology, healthcare, finance, etc.

- Within fixed-income, consider:

  - Government and Corporate Bonds: Diversify across issuers and maturities.

7. Consider Alternative Investments:

  - Explore alternative investments like real estate, commodities, or private equity to further diversify your portfolio.

  - Alternative investments may have a lower correlation with traditional asset classes.

8. Review and Rebalance Regularly:

  - Periodically review your portfolio to ensure it aligns with your target asset allocation.

  - Rebalance by selling over performing assets and buying underperforming ones to maintain the desired balance.

9. Factor in Market Conditions:

  - Adjust your portfolio based on prevailing market conditions and economic outlook.

- Be flexible in adapting to changing circumstances and opportunities in the market.

10. **Utilize Diversified Investment Vehicles:**

- Consider using investment vehicles that provide instant diversification, such as:

  - Exchange-Traded Funds (ETFs): Track an index and offer broad market exposure.

  - Mutual Funds: Managed funds that pool money from many investors to invest in a diversified portfolio.

11. **Risk Management and Monitoring:**

- Continuously monitor your portfolio's performance against your goals.

- Regularly assess risk factors and adjust your diversification strategy as needed.

12. **Seek Professional Advice if Necessary:**

- If you find creating a diversified portfolio challenging, consult with a financial advisor.

- A professional can provide personalized guidance based on your unique financial situation and goals.

By systematically diversifying your portfolio across various asset classes and investment types, you reduce the impact of market volatility on your overall returns. Diversification doesn't eliminate risk, but it is a powerful strategy to manage and navigate the complexities of the financial markets.

- Strategies for Long-Term Wealth Growth

Long-term wealth growth requires a strategic and disciplined approach to investing and financial management. Here are key strategies to consider for building and sustaining wealth over the long term:

1. **Start Early and Stay Consistent:**

- *Power of Compounding:* Time is a crucial factor in wealth creation. The earlier you start investing, the more time your money has to benefit from compounding returns.

  - *Consistent Contributions:* Regularly contribute to your investment accounts, even if the amounts are small initially. Consistency is key.

2. Set Clear Financial Goals:

  - *Define Objectives:* Clearly articulate your short-term and long-term financial goals. This could include milestones like homeownership, education funding, retirement, and more.

  - *Align Investments:* Align your investment strategy with your goals to ensure they are working together.

3. Diversify Your Portfolio:

  - *Asset Allocation:* Diversify across different asset classes (stocks, bonds, real estate, etc.) to spread risk.

  - *Regular Rebalancing:* Periodically rebalance your portfolio to maintain the desired asset allocation.

4. Invest for the Long Term:

- *Avoid Market Timing:* Resist the temptation to time the market. Long-term investing is about staying invested through market fluctuations.

- *Hold Quality Investments:* Invest in fundamentally sound companies with growth potential. Quality investments tend to perform well over time.

5. Maximize Tax-Efficiency:

- *Utilize Tax-Advantaged Accounts:* Contribute to tax-advantaged accounts like 401(k)s, IRAs, and HSAs to minimize tax liabilities.

- *Tax-Efficient Investments:* Consider tax-efficient investment strategies to optimize after-tax returns.

6. Embrace Dollar-Cost Averaging:

- *Systematic Investment:* Invest a fixed amount at regular intervals, regardless of market conditions. This strategy helps average out the cost of your investments over time.

7. Emergency Fund and Adequate Insurance:

- *Financial Safety Net:* Maintain an emergency fund to cover unforeseen expenses and avoid tapping into long-term investments.

- *Insurance Coverage:* Ensure you have adequate insurance coverage for health, life, and property to protect against financial setbacks.

8. Continuous Learning and Adjustment:

- *Stay Informed:* Stay abreast of financial news, economic trends, and changes in the investment landscape.

- *Adapt to Changes:* Adjust your investment strategy as needed based on changes in your financial situation, goals, and market conditions.

9. Real Estate Investment:

- *Property Ownership:* Consider real estate as a long-term investment. Property values tend to appreciate over time, and rental income can provide a steady cash flow.

- Diversification: Real estate can offer diversification beyond traditional investment classes.

10. Regularly Contribute to Retirement Accounts:

- Maximize Contributions: Contribute the maximum allowable amounts to retirement accounts like 401(k)s and IRAs to take advantage of tax benefits.

- Employer Matches: Take full advantage of employer-sponsored retirement plans and any employer matches offered.

11. Avoid High Levels of Debt:

- Manage Debt Wisely: While some debt may be necessary, avoid accumulating high-interest debt. Prioritize paying down debts to free up more funds for investing.

12. **Plan for Inflation:**

- *Inflation-Adjusted Investments:* Invest in assets that have the potential to outpace inflation over the long term. Consider inflation-protected securities and equities.

13. **Estate Planning:**

- *Create a Will:* Develop a comprehensive estate plan, including a will and other legal documents.

- *Tax-Efficient Wealth Transfer:* Explore strategies for tax-efficient wealth transfer to heirs.

14. **Review and Adjust:**

- *Regular Financial Checkups:* Periodically review your financial plan and adjust it based on changes in your life, goals, and the economic environment.

Long-term wealth growth is a dynamic process that requires a combination of strategic planning, disciplined saving, and informed investing. By implementing these strategies and staying committed to your financial goals, you can build and sustain wealth throughout your lifetime.

CHAPTER 4:
REALIZING YOUR
DREAMS

Welcome to the transformative journey encapsulated in Chapter 4: "Realizing Your Dreams." This chapter is a pivotal exploration into the actionable steps and mindset shifts needed to turn your aspirations into tangible reality. Realizing your dreams is not just about wishful thinking; it's about cultivating a proactive approach to set goals, overcome challenges, and live a life aligned with your deepest desires.

In the chapters preceding this, we've delved into the foundations of financial wisdom, the intricacies of investing, and the strategies for long-term wealth growth. Now, "Realizing Your Dreams" serves as the culmination of these efforts, guiding you through the practical steps and empowering insights required to manifest the life you envision.

This chapter goes beyond financial acumen, delving into the realms of personal development, goal-setting, and the mindset shifts necessary to break free from limitations. Whether your dreams involve financial independence, career milestones, personal growth, or a blend of these aspirations, the tools and wisdom found in this chapter will serve as your compass on this exhilarating journey.

Get ready to embark on a chapter dedicated to turning your dreams from distant aspirations into actionable plans. Through the stories of those who have achieved remarkable feats and the strategies designed to unlock your full potential, "Realizing Your Dreams" is your guide to carving a path toward a life of purpose, fulfilment, and accomplishment. Join me as we explore the profound intersection of dreams and reality, where the extraordinary becomes attainable, and your aspirations take center stage.

- Aligning Your Finances with Your Life Goals

Aligning your finances with your life goals is a crucial step towards achieving a fulfilling and purpose-driven existence. By integrating your financial strategy with your aspirations, you create a roadmap that directs your efforts towards the realization of your dreams. Here's a comprehensive guide on the process of aligning your finances with your life goals:

1. *- Personal and Financial Aspirations:*
Consider your short-term and long-term life goals. These could include homeownership, education, travel, starting a business, or retirement.

- Prioritize Goals: Rank your goals in terms of importance and urgency.

2. Quantify Your Goals:

- *Financial Estimation:* Attach a financial value to each goal. This involves estimating the cost associated with achieving your aspirations.

- *Time Horizon:* Define the timeframes for each goal, whether they are short-term goals within a few years or long-term goals spanning decades.

3. Create a Comprehensive Budget:

- *Income and Expenses:* Evaluate your current income and expenses. Ensure that your income comfortably covers your essential living expenses.

- *Allocate Funds:* Allocate a portion of your budget to each life goal. Prioritize funding for necessities, followed by discretionary spending aligned with your goals.

4. Build an Emergency Fund:

- *Financial Security:* Establish and maintain an emergency fund equivalent to three to six months of living expenses. This fund acts as a financial safety net, allowing you to navigate unexpected setbacks without derailing your goals.

5. Debt Management:

- *Prioritize High-Interest Debt:* If you have outstanding debts, prioritize paying off high-interest debts to free up funds for goal attainment.

- *Strategic Repayment Plans:* Develop a debt repayment plan that aligns with your budget and doesn't hinder progress towards your life goals.

6. Invest in Your Goals:

- *Strategic Investing:* Invest in assets that align with your goals and time horizon. For short-term goals, focus on less volatile investments, while long-term goals can accommodate a more diversified and growth-oriented portfolio.

- *Retirement Planning:* Contribute regularly to retirement accounts to ensure financial security in your later years.

7. **Utilize Tax-Advantaged Accounts:**

- *Maximize Contributions:* Take full advantage of tax-advantaged accounts such as 401(k)s, IRAs, and HSAs to minimize tax liabilities and boost savings.

- *Tax Planning:* Explore tax-efficient strategies to optimize your overall financial position.

8. **Regularly Review and Adjust:**

- *Periodic Assessments:* Regularly review your financial plan to ensure it aligns with your evolving goals, lifestyle, and economic conditions.

- *Adjustments:* Make adjustments as needed, especially in response to life changes, new goals, or shifts in your financial situation.

9. **Insurance Coverage:**

- **Risk Mitigation:** Ensure you have adequate insurance coverage, including health, life, and property insurance, to mitigate financial risks and protect against setbacks.

10. Engage in Professional Financial Advice:

- *Consult with a Financial Advisor:* Seek advice from a financial advisor to receive personalized guidance based on your unique goals, risk tolerance, and financial situation.

- *Investment Strategies:* Discuss investment strategies that align with your aspirations and risk profile.

11. Behavioral and Mindset Shifts:

- *Financial Mindset:* Cultivate a positive financial mindset that supports your goals. Challenge limiting beliefs and adopt a growth-oriented perspective.

- *Behavioral Adjustments:* Make conscious choices that align with your financial and life goals. Avoid impulsive financial decisions that may hinder progress.

12. **Celebrate Milestones:**

- *Acknowledgment:* Celebrate achievements and milestones along the way. Recognizing progress reinforces positive financial habits and motivates continued effort.

Aligning your finances with your life goals is an ongoing and dynamic process that requires continuous attention and adaptation. By integrating your financial strategy with your aspirations and making intentional decisions, you create a harmonious relationship between your financial well-being and the life you envision.

- Turning Passion into Profit

Turning passion into profit is a rewarding journey that involves leveraging your interests and skills to create a sustainable source of income. While it requires dedication and strategic planning, the fulfilment that comes from aligning your work with your passions can be immensely gratifying. Here's a comprehensive guide on the process of turning passion into profit:

1. Identify Your Passion:

- *Self-Reflection:* Reflect on your interests, hobbies, and activities that bring you joy and fulfilment.

- *Skills Assessment:* Identify the skills and expertise you've developed in areas you are passionate about.

2. Market Research:

- *Identify Niche Opportunities:* Research market trends and identify niche opportunities within your passion. Explore areas where your unique skills and interests can fill a gap in the market.

- *Competitor Analysis:* Study competitors to understand their strengths, and weaknesses, and how you can differentiate your offering.

3. Validate Your Idea:

- *Seek Feedback:* Share your passion project or business idea with friends, family, and potential target customers. Gather feedback to refine and validate your concept.

- *Test the Market:* Consider launching a pilot or testing the market with a smaller-scale version of your product or service.

4. Develop a Business Plan:

- *Define Your Vision and Mission:* Clearly articulate the purpose and goals of your venture.

- *Target Audience:* Identify your target audience and understand their needs and preferences.

- *Monetization Strategy:* Outline how you plan to generate revenue, whether through product sales, services, subscriptions, or other income streams.

- *Financial Projections:* Develop realistic financial projections to guide your business decisions.

5. Build Your Brand:

- *Brand Identity:* Create a strong brand identity that reflects your passion and resonates with your target audience.

- *Online Presence:* Establish a professional online presence through a website and social media. Use these platforms to showcase your passion and connect with your audience.

6. Monetize Your Passion:

- *Products and Services:* Develop and offer products or services related to your passion. This could include physical goods, digital products, consulting, workshops, or other offerings.

- *Diversify Income Streams:* Explore multiple revenue streams to enhance financial stability. This could involve partnerships, affiliate marketing, or collaborations.

7. **Set Realistic Goals:**

- *Short-Term and Long-Term Objectives:* Define both short-term and long-term goals for your venture. Break down larger goals into manageable milestones.

- *Measurable Metrics:* Establish key performance indicators (KPIs) to measure the success of your passion project.

8. **Invest in Your Skills:**

- *Continuous Learning:* Stay abreast of industry trends and continuously enhance your skills. This investment in personal development can contribute to the growth of your venture.

9. **Networking and Collaboration:**

- *Connect with Like-Minded Individuals:* Network with others who share your passion. Attend events, join online communities, and engage in conversations to expand your network.

- *Collaborations:* Explore collaboration opportunities with other businesses or influencers in your niche.

10. Adaptability and Resilience:

- *Adapt to Changes:* Be flexible and adaptive to changes in the market or industry. Embrace innovation and be open to refining your approach.

- *Learn from Setbacks:* View setbacks as learning opportunities. Resilience is key to overcoming challenges and sustaining long-term success.

11. Marketing and Promotion:

- *Content Marketing:* Share your passion through content creation. Whether it's blog posts, videos, or social media, use content marketing to build an audience.

- *Authentic Storytelling:* Share your journey and the story behind your passion. Authenticity can resonate with your audience.

12. **Customer Engagement:**

- *Build Relationships:* Foster strong relationships with your customers. Respond to feedback, engage in conversations, and create a sense of community around your passion.

- *Customer Loyalty:* Focus on building customer loyalty by consistently delivering value and maintaining a high level of customer satisfaction.

13. **Scale Your Passion Business:**

- *Scalability Planning:* As your venture grows, plan for scalability. Consider how you can expand your offerings, reach a broader audience, or automate certain aspects of your business.

14. **Financial Management:**

- *Budgeting and Financial Planning:* Implement sound financial management practices. Keep track of expenses, revenue, and profits to ensure the financial sustainability of your venture.

15. Celebrate Success and Stay Passionate:

- *Acknowledge Achievements:* Celebrate milestones and accomplishments along the way. Recognize the progress you've made toward turning your passion into a profitable venture.

- *Maintain Passion:* Despite the business aspects, stay connected to your passion. Maintain the joy and enthusiasm that inspired you to embark on this journey.

Turning passion into profit is a dynamic process that requires a combination of creativity, strategic planning, and dedication. By aligning your passion with a solid business strategy, you can not only create a sustainable source of income but also find profound fulfilment in doing what you love.

- Balancing Ambition with Contentment

Balancing ambition with contentment is a delicate and often introspective process that involves reconciling the desire for achievement and progress with a sense of satisfaction and gratitude for the present. Striking this balance is crucial for mental well-being, fulfilment, and maintaining a healthy perspective on success. Here's a comprehensive guide on the process of balancing ambition with contentment:

1. Define Your Values and Priorities:

- *Reflect on Core Values:* Identify your core values and the aspects of life that matter most to you. This serves as a foundation for aligning your ambitions with what truly brings you contentment.

2. Set Clear Goals:

- *SMART Goals:* Establish specific, measurable, achievable, relevant, and time-bound goals. Clarity in your ambitions helps guide your efforts and prevents aimless striving.

3. Practice Gratitude:

- *Daily Reflection:* Cultivate a habit of gratitude by reflecting on the positive aspects of your life regularly. This helps foster contentment by acknowledging and appreciating what you have achieved.

4. Mindfulness and Present Awareness:

- *Live in the Present:* Practice mindfulness to stay present in the moment. This helps you appreciate current achievements and experiences rather than constantly yearning for future successes.

5. Celebrate Small Wins:

- *Acknowledge Achievements:* Recognize and celebrate small victories along the way. These moments of success contribute to a sense of accomplishment and contentment.

6. Cultivate Self-Awareness:

- *Regular Self-Reflection:* Engage in regular self-reflection to understand your motivations and desires. Being aware of your aspirations helps you balance them with contentment.

7. **Establish Boundaries:**

- *Work-Life Balance:* Set clear boundaries between work and personal life. Strive for a balance that allows you to pursue your ambitions without sacrificing your well-being and relationships.

8. **Embrace the Journey:**

- *Process over Outcome:* Focus on the journey rather than solely fixating on the end goal. Appreciate the learning, growth, and experiences gained along the way.

9. **Practice Self-Compassion:**

- *Accept Imperfections:* Understand that perfection is unattainable. Be compassionate towards yourself, acknowledging imperfections and learning from setbacks.

10. **Build Meaningful Relationships:**

- *Quality over Quantity:* Cultivate deep and meaningful connections with others. Meaningful relationships contribute significantly to feelings of contentment.

11. Reevaluate and Adjust Goals:

- Periodic Assessment: Regularly reassess your goals and ambitions. Are they still aligned with your values? Adjust as needed to ensure your pursuits contribute to your overall well-being.

12. Healthy Comparison:

- Compare with Yourself: Rather than comparing yourself to others, compare your current self to your past self. Recognize personal growth and improvements.

13. Practice Detachment:

- Detach from Outcomes: While setting goals is essential, detach your self-worth from the outcomes. Understand that challenges and setbacks are part of the journey.

14. Invest in Well-Being:

- Holistic Wellness: Prioritize your physical, mental, and emotional well-being. A healthy lifestyle contributes to an overall sense of contentment.

15. Seek Fulfillment in Contribution:

- *Service and Contribution:* Find fulfilment in contributing to others and the community. Acts of kindness and service can bring a profound sense of contentment.

16. Engage in Hobbies and Passions:

- *Balance Work and Play:* Dedicate time to hobbies and activities you love. This balance provides a holistic sense of achievement and joy.

17. Learn to Say No:

- *Prioritize Commitments:* Learn to say no to commitments that do not align with your goals or bring you contentment. Prioritize your time and energy.

18. Professional Development with Purpose:

- *Skill Enhancement:* Pursue professional development, but align it with your passion and purpose. Strive for growth that resonates with your values.

19. Regularly Reassess Your Values:

- *Evolution of Values:* Values can evolve over time. Periodically reassess and ensure that your ambitions align with your current values and priorities.

20. Embrace Change:

- *Adaptability:* Be open to adapting your ambitions as circumstances change. Flexibility contributes to a balanced and contented approach to life.

Balancing ambition with contentment is a continual process of self-discovery and adjustment. By integrating your goals with an appreciation for the present moment and cultivating a content mindset, you create a harmonious approach to success that is both fulfilling and sustainable.

CHAPTER 5: LEGACY AND BEYOND

Welcome to the final chapter of our journey together: "Legacy and Beyond." As we navigate the realms of wealth creation, personal development, and the pursuit of dreams, this chapter serves as a contemplative space to explore the lasting impact we can leave on the world and future generations. "Legacy and Beyond" delves into the profound concept of legacy—how our actions, values, and contributions can transcend our lifetimes and shape the world beyond our immediate existence.

In the preceding chapters, we've covered the essential elements of financial wisdom, investment insights, and the delicate balance between ambition and contentment. Now, as we turn our attention to the broader perspective of legacy, we embark on a reflective journey that transcends monetary wealth alone. Legacy encompasses the intangible wealth of values, principles, and the positive imprint we leave on the lives of others.

This chapter encourages you to ponder questions that transcend the financial realm: What values will you instill in those who follow? How will your actions echo through time? What mark will you leave on your community, society, and the world at large? "Legacy and Beyond" is a call to introspection, urging you to consider the impact you wish to have and the contributions that will endure beyond your lifetime.

From the wisdom of financial stewardship to the importance of personal growth, each chapter has been a stepping stone leading to this culminating exploration of legacy. Join me as we navigate the significance of leaving a lasting imprint—one that extends beyond the accumulation of wealth and encapsulates the essence of a life well-lived. Together, let's embark on a journey to discover the profound and enduring legacy you have the power to create.

- Estate Planning and Wealth Preservation

Estate planning is a crucial aspect of managing your wealth and ensuring a smooth transfer of assets to your heirs while minimizing tax implications. Beyond the financial components, it involves making decisions about your healthcare, guardianship for dependents, and the legacy you want to leave. Here's a comprehensive discussion on estate planning and wealth preservation:

1. **Understanding Estate Planning:**

   - *Comprehensive Approach:* Estate planning is a comprehensive process that involves organizing your affairs and assets to facilitate their efficient transfer to beneficiaries.

   - *Legal Documentation:* It typically includes the creation of legal documents such as wills, trusts, powers of attorney, and healthcare directives.

2. Key Components of Estate Planning:

- *Will:* A will outlines how you want your assets distributed after your death and can designate guardians for minor children.

- *Trusts:* Trusts can be established to manage and distribute assets according to specific instructions. They can also provide privacy and potentially reduce estate taxes.

- *Power of Attorney:* This document appoints someone to make financial decisions on your behalf if you become unable to do so.

- *Healthcare Directive:* Also known as a living will or advance directive, this outlines your preferences for medical treatment if you're unable to communicate.

3. Benefits of Estate Planning:

- *Wealth Preservation:* Effective estate planning helps preserve your wealth by minimizing taxes and ensuring a smooth transition of assets.

- *Family Harmony:* Clear instructions in your estate plan can reduce the potential for family conflicts over inheritances.

- *Minimizing Probate:* Proper planning can help minimize the time and costs associated with the probate process.

4. **Tax Considerations:**

- *Estate Tax:* Depending on the size of your estate, there may be federal and state estate taxes. Proper planning can help minimize these taxes.

- *Gift Tax:* Lifetime gifts can also be subject to taxation, and understanding gift tax limits is essential for effective wealth transfer.

5. **Reviewing and Updating:**

- *Life Changes:* Regularly review and update your estate plan, especially after significant life events such as marriage, divorce, births, or changes in financial status.

- *Tax Law Changes:* Stay informed about changes in tax laws that may impact your estate plan.

6. Charitable Giving:

- *Philanthropic Goals:* Estate planning provides an opportunity to include charitable giving in your legacy. Charitable trusts or bequests can be structured to align with your philanthropic goals.

7. Wealth Preservation Strategies:

- *Asset Protection:* Consider strategies to protect your assets from potential creditors or legal judgments.

- *Insurance:* Utilize life insurance and other forms of insurance to provide liquidity for estate taxes and other expenses.

8. Business Succession Planning:

- *Family Businesses:* If you own a family business, plan for its succession to ensure a smooth transition to the next generation.

- *Buy-Sell Agreements:* Implement buy-sell agreements to address the transfer of business interests upon certain events, such as the death of an owner.

9. Family Meetings:

- *Open Communication:* Consider holding family meetings to discuss your estate plan. Open communication can help manage expectations and avoid surprises.

10. Professional Guidance:

- *Estate Planning Attorney:* Work with an experienced estate planning attorney to ensure that your plan aligns with legal requirements and your specific goals.

- *Financial Advisor:* Collaborate with a financial advisor to integrate your estate plan with your overall financial strategy.

11. Digital Estate Planning:

- *Digital Assets:* Consider digital estate planning, including instructions for managing online accounts, social media, and other digital assets.

12. Living Trusts:

- *Avoiding Probate:* Living trusts can help avoid probate, providing privacy and potentially reducing the time and costs associated with the legal process.

13. Letter of Intent:

- *Personal Wishes:* Include a letter of intent detailing your wishes, instructions, and any sentiments you want to convey to your loved ones.

14. Long-Term Care Planning:

- *Healthcare Expenses:* Plan for potential long-term care expenses, including the possibility of needing nursing home care.

Estate planning is not a one-time event but an ongoing process that should adapt to changes in your life and the legal landscape. By taking a proactive and comprehensive approach to estate planning, you not only preserve your wealth but also ensure that your wishes are carried out and your legacy endures according to your vision. It's a vital component of responsible financial stewardship and a gift to your loved ones.

- Giving Back: Philanthropy and Social Impact

Giving back through philanthropy and social impact initiatives is a powerful means of creating positive change in communities and beyond. Whether through charitable donations, volunteering, or supporting social causes, individuals and organizations can play a significant role in addressing societal challenges. Here's a comprehensive discussion on philanthropy and social impact:

1. **Defining Philanthropy:**

- ***Purposeful Giving:*** Philanthropy involves the intentional and strategic allocation of resources—financial, time, or expertise—to promote the well-being of others and address societal issues.

2. **Forms of Philanthropy:**

- ***Financial Donations:*** Contributing money to charitable organizations, causes, or foundations.

- ***In-Kind Contributions:*** Donating goods, services, or expertise to support organizations or communities.

- ***Volunteerism:*** Actively engaging in hands-on efforts to contribute time and skills to a cause.

3. **Social Impact:**

- ***Purpose-Driven Initiatives:*** Social impact refers to the positive change generated by initiatives designed to address specific social challenges.

- *Measurable Outcomes:* Social impact efforts aim to achieve measurable outcomes that enhance the well-being of individuals and communities.

4. Individual and Corporate Philanthropy:

- *Individual Giving:* Personal philanthropy involves individuals contributing to causes they are passionate about.

- *Corporate Social Responsibility (CSR):* Companies engage in philanthropy and social impact as part of their commitment to ethical and responsible business practices.

5. Strategic Giving:

- *Identifying Causes:* Strategic philanthropy involves aligning giving with personal or organizational values and selecting causes that have a meaningful impact.

- *Long-Term Solutions:* Focusing on sustainable solutions rather than short-term fixes contributes to lasting change.

6. **Global and Local Impact:**

- *Global Philanthropy:* Addressing international issues and supporting global causes.

- *Local Community Support:* Contributing to the well-being of local communities through initiatives that address specific needs.

7. **Foundations and Nonprofits:**

- *Establishing Foundations:* Some individuals or families establish foundations to centralize and manage their philanthropic activities.

- *Nonprofit Organizations:* Supporting existing nonprofits that align with your values allows for the pooling of resources with like-minded individuals.

8. **Impact Investing:**

- *Financial Returns with Social Impact:* Impact investing involves making investments that generate financial returns while contributing to positive social and environmental outcomes.

- Sustainable Development Goals (SDGs):
Aligning investments with the United Nations'
SDGs to address global challenges.

9. **Social Entrepreneurship:**

- Business for Good: Social entrepreneurs create
businesses with a primary focus on addressing
social or environmental issues.

- Innovation for Impact: Developing innovative
solutions to societal challenges through
entrepreneurial endeavors.

10. **Measuring and Evaluating Impact:**

- Metrics and Evaluation: Establishing clear
metrics to measure the success and impact of
philanthropic and social impact initiatives.

- Continuous Improvement: Regularly evaluating
and refining strategies based on lessons learned.

11. Collaborative Philanthropy:

- *Partnerships:* Collaborating with other philanthropists, organizations, and stakeholders to amplify impact.

- *Collective Impact:* Working together towards shared goals for more significant and sustained outcomes.

12. Educating and Advocacy:

- *Raising Awareness:* Philanthropy extends beyond financial contributions to include educating others about important issues.

- *Advocacy and Policy Influence:* Engaging in advocacy efforts to address systemic issues and influence policy changes.

13. Challenges and Ethical Considerations:

- *Impact Assessment Challenges:* Measuring the true impact of philanthropy can be complex.

- Ethical Giving: Ensuring that philanthropic efforts adhere to ethical standards and do not unintentionally cause harm.

14. **Legacy Giving:**

- Endowments and Foundations: Establishing foundations or endowments to ensure a lasting legacy of impact.

- Multigenerational Philanthropy: Involving family members in philanthropic endeavors to pass down values and a commitment to social impact.

15. **Technology and Innovation:**

- Tech for Good: Leveraging technology and innovation for philanthropic purposes.

- Crowdsourced Philanthropy: Online platforms that allow individuals to contribute small amounts collectively for impactful causes.

16. Adaptability and Flexibility:

- *Responsive Giving:* Being adaptable to emerging needs and crises, and adjusting philanthropic strategies accordingly.

- *Learning and Iteration:* Embracing a learning mindset and iterating approaches based on evolving understanding.

Philanthropy and social impact represent a transformative force capable of addressing societal challenges, promoting equity, and fostering positive change. Whether on an individual or organizational level, the intentional and thoughtful allocation of resources towards philanthropic endeavors can leave a lasting legacy of compassion, empowerment, and social well-being.

- Sustaining Prosperity for Future Generations

Sustaining prosperity for future generations involves careful financial planning, responsible wealth management, and the cultivation of values that foster long-term success. To ensure that the benefits of prosperity extend beyond the present, consider the following comprehensive process:

1. Establish Clear Values and Principles:

- *Family Values:* Define the core values and principles that guide your family's approach to wealth and prosperity.

- *Ethical Framework:* Establish an ethical framework that ensures responsible financial stewardship.

2. Communication and Education:

- *Family Discussions:* Foster open communication about wealth, its responsibilities, and the family's financial goals.

- *Financial Literacy:* Invest in the financial education of family members, ensuring they understand wealth management principles.

3. *Develop a Comprehensive Financial Plan:*

- *Multi-Generational Planning:* Engage in multi-generational financial planning to align the family's financial goals with its values.

- *Long-Term Objectives:* Define clear long-term objectives for wealth preservation, growth, and distribution.

4. Asset Protection Strategies:

- *Legal Structures:* Consider the use of legal structures such as trusts and holding companies to protect assets.

- *Insurance Policies:* Implement insurance policies to safeguard against unforeseen risks and liabilities.

5. Teach Responsible Financial Behavior:

- *Financial Discipline:* Instill financial discipline by teaching prudent spending, saving, and investing habits.

- *Work Ethic:* Encourage a strong work ethic to foster a sense of purpose and responsibility.

6. Promote Entrepreneurship and Innovation:

- *Encourage Creativity:* Support entrepreneurial endeavors and innovative thinking within the family.

- *Business Ventures:* Explore opportunities for family members to engage in business ventures aligned with their passions and skills.

7. Diversification of Investments:

- *Asset Allocation:* Implement a well-diversified investment strategy to manage risk and optimize returns.

- *Adapt to Market Changes:* Stay informed about market trends and be willing to adapt investment portfolios based on changing economic conditions.

8. Tax Planning:

- *Minimize Tax Liabilities:* Engage in tax planning strategies to minimize the family's tax liabilities and maximize after-tax returns.

- *Stay Informed:* Stay informed about changes in tax laws and adjust financial strategies accordingly.

9. Encourage Philanthropy:

- *Social Responsibility:* Foster a sense of social responsibility by engaging in philanthropic initiatives.

- *Establish Foundations:* Consider creating family foundations to formalize and structure philanthropic activities.

10. Succession Planning:

- *Identify Successors:* Plan for the smooth transition of leadership roles within family businesses or wealth management.

- Professional Guidance: Seek the assistance of financial advisors and legal professionals to navigate succession planning complexities.

11. **Documenting Family Wealth Philosophy:**

- Family Constitution: Develop a family constitution that documents the family's wealth philosophy, values, and guiding principles.

- Success Stories: Share success stories and lessons learned to reinforce the family's commitment to sustained prosperity.

12. **Cultivate a Strong Governance Structure:**

- Family Governance: Establish a governance structure to facilitate decision-making, conflict resolution, and communication.

- Advisory Boards: Consider forming advisory boards to provide external perspectives and expertise.

13. Foster a Culture of Learning:

- *Continuous Education:* Encourage a culture of continuous learning, with an emphasis on adapting to changes in the financial landscape.

- *External Expertise:* Engage external experts, such as financial advisors and legal professionals, to provide specialized knowledge.

14. Plan for Contingencies:

- *Emergency Funds:* Maintain emergency funds to address unexpected financial challenges.

- *Risk Mitigation:* Develop contingency plans for potential economic downturns or disruptions.

15. *Environmental, Social, and Governance (ESG) Considerations:*

- *Sustainable Investing:* Integrate ESG considerations into investment decisions to align with environmental and social responsibility.

- *Corporate Responsibility:* Encourage family businesses to adopt sustainable and responsible business practices.

16. **Regular Family Meetings:**

- *Collaborative Decision-Making:* Conduct regular family meetings to facilitate collaborative decision-making and build a sense of shared responsibility.

- *Review and Reflect:* Use these meetings to review financial plans, assess progress, and reflect on the family's values.

17. **Preserve Family Stories and Traditions:**

- *Oral Histories:* Document family stories and traditions through oral histories, preserving the cultural and emotional wealth that extends beyond financial assets.

- *Legacy Preservation:* Ensure that future generations understand the family's history and the principles that have contributed to its prosperity.

Sustaining prosperity for future generations involves a multidimensional and intentional approach that goes beyond financial considerations. By combining strategic financial planning with the promotion of responsible behavior, educational initiatives, and a commitment to social and environmental responsibility, families can create a legacy of lasting prosperity that transcends generations.

CONCLUSION

In concluding our journey through "Get Rich Now: Secrets to Building Wealth and Living Your Dream Life," it is my sincere hope that the insights shared within these pages have ignited a spark of inspiration and empowerment within you. The pursuit of wealth is not merely about accumulating monetary assets but is a holistic journey encompassing personal growth, mindful financial management, and the realization of your deepest aspirations.

We've navigated the intricacies of financial wisdom, from mastering the basics of budgeting to delving into the world of investments. We've explored the profound impact of mindset on financial success, unravelling the psychology of wealth and unlocking the secrets to overcoming limiting beliefs. Throughout, the emphasis has been on cultivating not just wealth but a life rich in purpose, joy, and fulfilment.

As you stand at the threshold of your financial journey, armed with the knowledge and strategies shared in this book, remember that true wealth extends beyond bank balances. It is the ability to align your financial resources with your life goals, to balance ambition with contentment, and to leave a legacy that transcends generations.

Building wealth is not a sprint but a marathon—a journey that requires resilience, adaptability, and a commitment to continuous learning. It involves not just accumulating riches for oneself but leveraging prosperity to make a positive impact on the world. Whether you aspire to philanthropy, social entrepreneurship, or other avenues of giving back, the path to lasting wealth is paved to create a better future for yourself and those around you.

As you embark on this journey, keep in mind that wealth is a tool—an enabler of dreams and a means to make a difference. Your financial success is intertwined with your personal growth, your relationships, and your contribution to the well-being of others. May the secrets shared in these pages serve as a compass, guiding you toward a life of abundance, purpose, and fulfilment?

In closing, I encourage you to approach your financial endeavors with intention, wisdom, and a generous spirit. Embrace the opportunities to learn, grow, and adapt. Your dream life awaits, and with the right mindset and strategic approach, you have the power to not only get rich but to live a life that reflects your deepest aspirations. Here's to your journey of wealth, well-being, and the realization of your dreams. May it be truly extraordinary?

www.ingramcontent.com/pod-product-compliance
Lightning Source LLC
Chambersburg PA
CBHW072331290526
45794CB00002B/826